To the Extreme

Kickboxing

by Angie Peterson Kaelberer

Reading Consultant:
Barbara J. Fox
Reading Specialist
North Carolina State University

Capstone press

Mankato, Minnesota

Blazers is published by Capstone Press,
151 Good Counsel Drive, P.O. Box 669, Mankato, Minnesota 56002.
www.capstonepress.com

Library of Congress Cataloging-in-Publication Data
Kaelberer, Angie Peterson.
    Kickboxing / by Angie Peterson Kaelberer.
    p. cm.—(Blazers. To the extreme)
    Summary: "Describes the sport of kickboxing, including
techniques, rules, competitions, and safety information"—Provided
by publisher.
    Includes bibliographical references and index.
    ISBN 0-7368-4399-X (hardcover)
    1. Kickboxing—Juvenile literature. I. Title. II. Series.
GV1114.65.K34 2006
796.815—dc22   2005001434

Credits
Jason Knudson, set designer; Kate Opseth, book designer; Jo Miller,
    photo researcher; Scott Thoms, photo editor

Photo Credits
AP/Wide World Photos/Keystone, Markus Stuecklin, 14, 25
Art Directors/Peter Treanor, 27
Corbis/TempSport, Franck Seguin, cover, 5, 6, 8, 8–9, 9, 11, 13,
    16–17, 24, 28–29
Getty Images Inc./AFP/Mehdi Fedouach, 12, 19; John Gichigi, 23;
    Liaison/Paula Bronstein, 26; Mike Powell, 15
Globe Photos Inc./Victor B. Maldonada, 20

**Capstone Press thanks Mike Miles, National Kickboxing and Muay
Thai, Calgary, Alberta, Canada, for his assistance with this book.**

1 2 3 4 5 6 10 09 08 07 06 05

Table of Contents

Kicking with Power

Two kickboxers face each other
in a ring. The challenger throws a
punch. The champion prepares to
strike back with a high kick.

Ropes

The challenger bounces off the ropes. The boxers trade sharp jabs to the head.

BLAZER FACT

Kickboxing was first called full-contact karate.

The champion raises his left leg
for a side kick. He follows with a kick
of his right leg and another with the
left. The bell rings. The round is over.

Moves

Kickboxers can use their
feet to attack an opponent.
They do side kicks, turn kicks,
and roundhouse kicks.

Roundhouse kick

Jabs

Punches are also part of kickboxing. Boxers use jabs, uppercuts, crosses, and hooks.

Uppercut punch

Kickboxers use blocks to defend themselves. They learn to block both punches and kicks.

Kickboxing Diagram

Side kick

Ring rope

Anklet

Boxing gloves

Mat

safety

All kickboxers wear boxing
gloves. They wrap their hands with
tape before they put on the gloves.

Foot pad

Shin pad

In the United States, kickboxers protect their legs and feet with shin pads and foot pads. Boxers in other countries don't have to wear pads.

BLAZER FACT

Kicks begin with a move called chambering. Boxers bring their knee to their chest to start the kick.

Competitions

Most U.S. competitions use American full-contact rules. Boxers must kick at least eight times during each round. No kicks are allowed below the waist.

In international competitions,
boxers aim kicks almost anywhere
on the body. They can use their
knees to strike opponents.

Kickboxing is popular all over the world. Muay Thai kickboxing began in Thailand. Muay Thai allows punches, kicks, knee strikes, and elbow jabs.

BLAZER FACT

Competitions have separate matches for men and women.

Landing a roundhouse kick!

Glossary

challenger (CHAL-uhnj-uhr)—a kickboxer who competes against a champion

chambering (CHAYM-bur-ing)—to bring the knee up to the chest; every kick begins with this move.

champion (CHAM-pee-uhn)—the winner of a kickboxing competition or title

international (in-tur-NASH-uh-nuhl)—including more than one country

karate (kah-RAH-tee)—a martial art using controlled kicks and punches

Muay Thai (MOO-ay TYE)—a form of kickboxing that began in Thailand

opponent (uh-POH-nuhnt)—a person who competes against another person

Read More

Collins, Paul. *Muay Thai: Thai Boxing.* Martial Arts. Broomall, Penn.: Chelsea House, 2002.

Mitchell, David. *Martial Arts.* DK Superguides. New York: Dorling Kindersley, 2000.

Nonnemacher, Klaus. *Kickboxing.* Martial Arts. Milwaukee: Gareth Stevens, 2005.

Sievert, Terri. *Kickboxing.* X-Sports. Mankato, Minn.: Capstone Press, 2005.

Internet Sites

FactHound offers a safe, fun way to find Internet sites related to this book. All of the sites on FactHound have been researched by our staff.

Here's how:

1. Visit *www.facthound.com*
2. Type in this special code **073684399X** for age-appropriate sites. Or enter a search word related to this book for a more general search.
3. Click on the **Fetch It** button.

FactHound will fetch the best sites for you!

Index